ISBN: 978129025107

Published by:
HardPress Publishing
8345 NW 66TH ST #2561
MIAMI FL 33166-2626

Email: info@hardpress.net
Web: http://www.hardpress.net

OVER THE MISTY MOUNTAINS. PAST THE WIDE HEIGHTS OF BLUE · EVEN TO THE CRYSTAL FOUNTAINS · WHERE ALL THE DREAMS COME TRUE"

"ONE EVERLASTING WHISPER
DAY AND NIGHT REPEATED—SO:
'SOMETHING HIDDEN · GO AND
FIND IT · GO AND LOOK BEHIND
THE RANGES—SOMETHING LOST
BEHIND THE RANGES · LOST
AND WAITING FOR YOU · GO!'"

THE MOUNTAIN TRAIL AND ITS MESSAGE

"*He leadeth me in the paths of righteousness.*" — PSALMS 23: 3.

GILMORE LAKE, SIERRA NEVADA

THE MOUNTAIN TRAIL AND ITS MESSAGE

BY

ALBERT W. PALMER

THE PILGRIM PRESS
BOSTON NEW YORK CHICAGO

THE · PLIMPTON · PRESS
[W · D · O]
NORWOOD · MASS · U · S · A

HETCH-HETCHY VALLEY

THE MOUNTAIN TRAIL AND ITS MESSAGE

IT has been my privilege during the month of my summer vacation for the last three years to be led in paths — paths which have been to me paths of righteousness, of joy, and of inspiration. Out here in the West we call these paths mountain trails. It is out of my experience with these "paths of righteousness" that I seek to bring you the message of the mountain trail.

The trail is not the grandest thing in the mountains — it is only a humble path. It is not the most beautiful — it is often ugly and scarred, filled with dust and stones. But it is one of the absolutely necessary things, and one comes into a peculiar intimacy with it. There is a vast difference between a trail and a road. There are usually many roads, and if one loses the road he may make inquiries and find another one. But if one loses the trail he must find that one trail again, and there is no one of whom to ask directions. A road advertises itself afar off. You can always tell when you are coming to a road, but you may pass within twenty feet of a mountain trail and never dream of its presence, so modest is it and so slight. A road looks very much alike mile after mile, but every rod of a mountain trail has its individuality all its own. One usually travels a road in a vehicle, but I have always traveled the mountain trail on foot, and, traveling so, every rise, every down grade, every stretch of dusty sunshine, every cool shadow becomes important and noteworthy. And so, as day by day you surrender yourself to the mountain trail and follow gladly where it leads, there comes a feeling of peculiar intimacy and companionship with it.

My experiences on the mountain trail have been, for the most part, in connection with the annual outings of the Sierra Club. Our outing parties number from one hundred twenty to two hundred people and we spend a month each summer in some remote and beautiful part of the Sierra Nevada. All supplies are carried by our hired pack train of mules and horses over mountain trails, for we go into that region where the roads "run out and stop." At night we sleep in the open air in sleeping bags on piles of fir boughs or pine needles or even, after a hard day's tramp, gratefully upon the hard clean ground. Each person is limited to forty pounds of baggage, which must include sleeping bag, extra clothing, and all personal belongings. This forty pounds must be packed in a dunnage bag three feet long and eighteen inches in diameter, with the owner's name blazoned on the side in letters two inches high.

The cooking is done by Charlie Tuck, a Chinaman of the type that every true Californian loves even as a Southerner loves his old "Uncle 'Rastus." In the winter he cooks for a hotel in San Rafael, but his Heathen Chinee soul is not indifferent to the call of the wild, for in his hotel contract he always specifies that he is to have July free to go with the Sierra Club. He has two Japanese and his nephew, Toy, as helpers and he rules "the commissary," as the camp kitchen is called, as supremely as ever the Empress Dowager ruled Peking. It is stern and simple fare he gives us — soup and rice and canned corn and tomatoes, fresh meat occasionally, trout in abundance, hard-tack, bacon, dried prunes and figs, and, on high days and holidays, a white pasty pudding, with infrequent raisins scattered through it, which the irreverent have nick-named "Wall-paperer's Delight."

Our party is made up of lawyers, doctors, college professors, high school teachers, and occasionally a rancher, business man, or minister. There are even more temperaments and points of view than occupations. The mountains seem to mean something different to each one. There is my nephew, the Fisherman — he values each camp in terms of the number of trout that rise to his fly in the adjacent mountain torrent. The Geologist loafs along the trail, oblivious to the very existence of trout, breaking rocks with his hammer, and, after everyone else is in camp, the Botanist drifts wearily in, like an overdue tramp steamer through the Golden Gate, with his press full of flowers. No ancient lava or rainbow trout for his herbarium, if you please! This man in the well-tailored khaki suit has been planning reservoir sites all day and that other man in shabby corduroys and a broad gray hat has been watching the shadows in the canyons, listening to the music in the trees, and entering into fellowship with the chipmunks that cheerily share his lunch.

And then, when the day's tramp of from six to eighteen miles is over, we all gather after supper in a great circle around the camp-fire. Each member of the party contributes according to his ability. There are silent souls that do their share by keeping the fire a-blazing, there is a Los Angeles lawyer with an improvised limerick for every occasion and a Berkeley doctor with an inexhaustible supply of stories. The Botanist and the Geologist share their knowledge with the rest of us, leaving out the big words, and a quartet, four men from four corners of the country, sing some of the good old songs. Last of all "the Signor," with his head thrown back and his fine spiritual face illumined by the blazing fire, touches his violin and pours out in music the things we all long to say and cannot.

Sunday comes and we gather, men and women of many creeds

or no creed at all, under the shelter of some majestic yellow pine with the great cliffs towering above us. The old hymns, led by the violin, the simple prayer, the Twenty-third Psalm repeated together, the sermon touched with a sense of the Divine presence all around us — these things all help to make a summer in the Sierra more than a physical refreshment alone.

And so by day we live in fellowship with the trees, ever calm, dignified, serene, and with the great cliffs in whose presence we feel so slight and so transitory. And then at night, when the camp-fire has died away and a hush has settled down across the hills, we lie in our sleeping bags and, before we close our eyes, look straight up at the innumerable and silent stars, and learn anew what it may mean to pray.

Last year a member of our Sierra Club wrote a very beautiful little poem entitled "The Mountain Trail." It has not yet been published and I am not at liberty to reproduce it in print. It tells of how the trail winds its way up the mountain side, through the flower-strewn mountain meadows, across the rushing rivers, up the great rock slopes, and even over the gleaming snow, and closes with the longing that it may go on forever.

"Over the misty mountains,
Past the wide heights of blue,
Even to the crystal fountains,
Where all the dreams come true."

I do not wonder that the mountain trail should arouse a poet to song, for I have spent days on the mountain trail which were in themselves like poems lived, and the memory of which is like the echo of some great music. I have started out in the morning and climbed a rocky, dusty trail up steep zig-zags through the chaparral until, hot and weary, I have come to a gently sloping plateau land, where the trail wound slowly upward through fragrant pines with great bronzed trunks and then dipped into little meadows green with spring-time and glad with flowers. In the trees birds were singing, and as I listened I said over to myself those beautiful lines of Edwin Markham's on "Joy in the Morning":

"I hear you, little bird,
Shouting a-swing above the broken wall.
Shout louder yet; no song can tell it all.
Sing to my soul in the deep, still wood;
'Tis wonderful beyond the wildest word;
I'd tell it, too, if I could."

And then I have climbed up above the tree line and, sitting beside a bed of white heather with its exquisite white and crimson bells, have looked across the jagged peaks and gleaming snow drifts of the summit region. Below, a blue little lake with solemn trees around it; yonder, a lake still frozen over, with a snow bank reaching down to it like a miniature glacier; and everywhere the beautiful French-gray granite cliffs, so clean that they make one feel as if all sin and stain had been swept from this upper world forever. And then I have crossed the pass and gone down the other side, reached camp, and again felt the joy of companionship and home.

1. I find in the mountain trail many parables, but first of all a parable of the higher life. The mountain trail life involves hardship. The trail is far beyond the reach of wagon roads. No luxurious cars carry one around its

curves. No one leans back on the cushions of an automobile along the mountain trail. He who would know the trail must leave the comforts and luxuries of civilization behind, must be glad to wear great heavy hob-nailed shoes, strong simple clothing, must be ready to live laborious days, to lie down at night weary on the hard ground, to eat plain food and to share in the hard work of camp life.

If a man will do this the trail shall bring him great rewards — a clear atmosphere such as the valley people never know, the beauty and majesty of mountain fastnesses which the people in the luxurious trains see not, and, when the roads where the great automobiles speed along are lined with dust and sunburned grass, the trail will lead him into little nooks where the flowers are yet in spring time.

Is not this a parable of life?

There are men who live their lives on the wagon roads, in the Pullman car, on the cushions of an automobile. They shun all hardship, their object in life is to avoid all pain, just to have a good time. And they have their reward — miles of dusty road, acres of sunburned grass.

But there are other men who live the life of the mountain trail, the life of aspiration and endeavor. They are

"Pioneer souls who blaze their paths
Where the highways never ran."

They hear something calling them out of the unseen even as Kipling's Explorer heard

"One everlasting Whisper day and night repeated — so:
'Something hidden. Go and find it. Go and look behind the Ranges —
Something lost behind the Ranges. Lost and waiting for you. Go!'"

They, therefore, consecrate themselves not to the common dusty roads of material comfort and pleasure, but to the quest of the ideal.

It means oftentimes a loss of comfort, it means poverty perchance, it may mean defeat, as the world counts defeat, to follow this trail of the ideal. But it is the men who have lived such lives who have moved the world, and they have not been without their reward — beautiful flowers bloom for them which the men on the dusty road below know not of.

I have found myself this summer often thinking of Jesus' saying, "I am the way." What a splendid trail of the ideal his life has blazed across the mountains of this life! What joy of the mountaineer comes to those who follow in that trail!

2. The trail also brings to me a parable of our indebtedness to the past. No man can walk mile after mile over a mountain trail without a feeling of gratitude toward the men who made it. Resting beside the trail one day I found myself thinking of the Indians who first found the pass; of the rough pioneer soldiers under Kit Carson or some other fearless leader who may have been the first white men over the route; of the cattle men who made it easier and plainer; of John Muir in his rugged youth, traveling alone with his flour and his tea, and without blankets that he might carry more food and thus be able to penetrate farther into the fastnesses of the Sierra and bring back to the people word of the wonders and beauties he had seen. I thought also of the foresters who had re-

built the trail and of the troopers who guarded it. Into a sense of grateful fellowship with all these men one enters as he lives day by day in companionship with the mountain trail — this long slender thread which, stretching back over the hills, seems to be the only thing connecting him with civilization and, leading on into the unknown, promises new joy and beauty for the days to come.

And with this gratitude goes a duty — the duty not in any way to injure the trail, but, as far as possible, so to place a stone here or remove one there as to improve the trail and make it plainer and easier. In high altitudes the trail goes over the bare granite, where there is no way of marking its location except by low piles of stones, called "ducks," placed at frequent intervals. It is an unwritten law of the mountains never to destroy a "duck," but, rather, to add another stone.

What a parable it is of our heritage of human institutions and ideas! These customs and institutions are the trails across the mountains of time builded by the men who went before us. The family, the state, the Church, law, religion, standards of honor and conduct — they are all great trails to find and mark which our ancestors ever since before the dawn of history have labored.

How wise the man who treats these things in the spirit in which the mountaineer treats the trail!

The true mountaineer does not start off cross country regardless of trails. He knows difficulties and dangers will confront him if he does. It may seem strange that the trail goes down here or up there, but he stays by it because he knows that the men who built the trail must have had reasons for their course. And so he follows the trail and sees that it is in no way injured or obscured. More than that, he improves the trail. He realizes that no trail is perfect. He puts a log across a bad stream crossing, and if a tree has fallen across the trail he chops a way through it or around it. He may even, with better surveying instruments and with dynamite to blast the rocks, find and build a shorter and better grade. But through it all the old trail is the basis on which he works, and he never forgets or despises the men who made it.

Happy the man who follows this parable in regard to human ideas and institutions; who seeks not to destroy but to fulfil; who, when he seeks to reform the social order, realizes the heroic service that was given to bring to pass even the imperfect freedom and justice we have today; who, when he criticises the Church, appreciates also the work it has done and is doing for the world; who, when he reaches a sweeter and simpler creed, remembers that the creeds of the past, however rough and crude and harsh, were yet trails over which men traveled on to fellowship with God.

3. Again there comes to me a message from the companionship of the trail. No man passes any other upon the trail without speaking to him. Strangers will stop and exchange information about good camping places. The standards of value and judgment are different from those on the great roads below. Men are not valued

according to their wealth at home. No one cares who your father was or what club you belong to. Neither is judgment based on outward appearances. The man with the shiniest shoes or newest fangled kind of knapsack is not the man most honored on the trail.

The trail has different standards. It honors and respects and yields obedience to character and the capacity and willingness to do. The man who does his share of the work without grumbling, the man who does the cooking (though he be a man with eyes aslant and a cue hidden under his old hat), the man who contributes his talents to the common good modestly and cheerfully, whether his particular talent be catching trout, telling a good story, running the pack train, frying hot cakes, or playing a violin in the light of the camp-

HETCH-HETCHY
VALLEY

LITTLE KERN
LAKE

HEAD OF TUOLUMNE CANYON

MT. FLORENCE
TUOLUMNE MEADOWS AND FAIRVIEW DOME

fire so that the cliffs echo back such music as they never heard before — whatever the talent may be, there is the man who is honored and respected on the trail.

And if but one humble and obscure man on a mountain trail be lost, every other man on the trail feels in duty bound to aid in the search till the lost is found. One night two of our party failed to come into camp. As searchers started out on horseback how gladly we contributed little articles which might be of service! How anxiously we waited until an hour later two shots far down the canyon told us that both the lost ones had been found!

What a magnificent thing if we could bring this companionship and these standards down into the city street!

How fine to keep up that feeling

of brotherhood which, in the spirit of Walt Whitman, silently at least, salutes every man we meet! How fine to keep on judging people, not by their clothes or their wealth or social standing, but by character! How fine if we could awaken in the great roaring city, with its saloons, its brothels, its gambling dens, that mountain responsibility for seeking and finding those who go astray!

4. There is a fourth lesson of the trail. It is one which John Muir taught me. There are always some people in the mountains who are known as "hikers." They rush over the trail at high speed and take great delight in being the first to reach camp and in covering the greatest number of miles in the least possible time. They measure the trail in terms of speed and distance.

One day as I was resting in the shade Mr. Muir overtook me on the trail and began to chat in that friendly way in which he delights to talk with everyone he meets. I said to him: "Mr. Muir, someone told me you did not approve of the word 'hike,' is that so?" His blue eyes flashed, and with his Scotch accent he replied: "I don't like either the word or the thing. People ought to saunter in the mountains — not 'hike!' Do you know the origin of that word saunter? It's a beautiful word. Away back in the middle ages people used to go on pilgrimages to the Holy Land, and when people in the villages through which they passed asked where they were going they would reply, 'A la sainte terre,' 'To the Holy Land.' And so they became known as sainte-terre-ers or saunterers. Now these mountains are our Holy Land, and we ought to saunter through them reverently, not 'hike' through them." And John Muir lived up to his doctrine. He was usually the last man to reach camp. He never hurried. He stopped to get acquainted with individual trees along the way, he would hail people passing by and make them get down on hands and knees if necessary to examine some tiny seedling or to see the beauty of some little bed of almost microscopic flowers. Usually he appeared at camp with some new flowers in his hat and a little piece of fir bough in his button-hole.

Now, whether the derivation of saunter just given is scientific or fanciful, is there not in it another parable? There are people who "hike" through life. They measure life in terms of money and amusement; they rush along the trail of life feverishly seeking to make a dollar or gratify an appetite. How much better to "saunter" along this trail of life, to measure it in terms of beauty and love and friendship! How much finer to take time to know and understand the men and women along the way, to stop a while and let the beauty of the sunset possess the soul, to listen to what the trees are saying and the songs of the birds, and to gather the fragrant little flowers that bloom all along the trail of life for those who have eyes to see!

You can't do these things if you rush through life in a big red automobile at high speed; you can't know these things if you "hike" along the trail in a speed competition. These are the peculiar rewards of the man who has learned the secret of the saunterer!

5. There is one last parable which the mountain trail brings to me — its endlessness. It climbs to the crest of the ridge and is lost to sight, but it goes down the other side. It loses itself in the green depths of the canyons below, but far away on the other wall, if your eyes are clear and strong, you can make it out zig-zagging up out of the canyon again. You camp for the night weary beside the trail, but the trail runs on as a prophecy that you too shall follow in the morning. Only once have I followed a mountain trail to its end, and that was when we climbed Mt. Whitney. There, fourteen thousand five hundred feet above sea level, at the very highest point in the United States, the trail seemed to end at a rude pile of

stones. But do you know I believe the poet saw the deeper truth, and I too believe that there is a trail that still leads on

"Over the misty mountains,
Past the wide heights of blue,
Even to the crystal fountains,
Where all the dreams come true."

"ONE EVERLASTING WHISPER
DAY AND NIGHT REPEATED—SO:
'SOMETHING HIDDEN · GO AND
FIND IT · GO AND LOOK BEHIND
THE RANGES—SOMETHING LOST
BEHIND THE RANGES · LOST
AND WAITING FOR YOU · GO!'"

"OVER THE MISTY MOUNTAINS,
PAST THE WIDE HEIGHTS OF
BLUE · EVEN TO THE CRYSTAL
FOUNTAINS · WHERE ALL
THE DREAMS COME TRUE"

CPSIA information can be obtained at www.ICGtesting.com
Printed in the USA
LVOW04s0358131015

458026LV00028B/446/P

9 781290 251075